COLOR & LEARN

COLORING BOOK FOR KIDS

FLOWERS

To my beautiful and talented daughter, Ameena.

Follow the instructions below to see the pictures come to life!

1. Download Overly app

over.ly/get

2. Open the app and use your camera to scan the whole picture

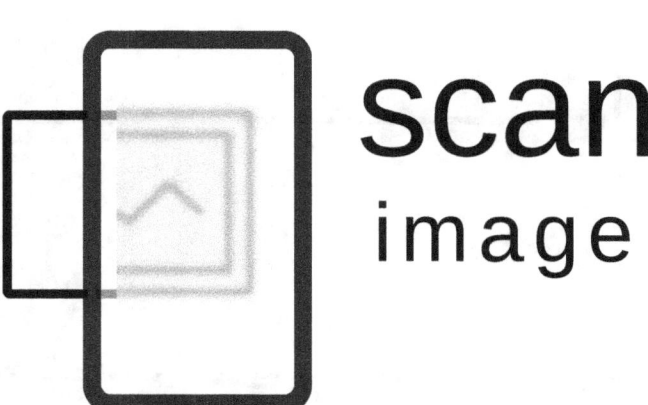

scan image

3. Watch the magic happen with augmented reality!

view magic

THIS BOOK BELONGS TO:

_____

Rose

A red rose
means love.

Carnation

Color a white
carnation by putting
dye in the vase water.

Daffodil

Daffodils are also called Narcissus.

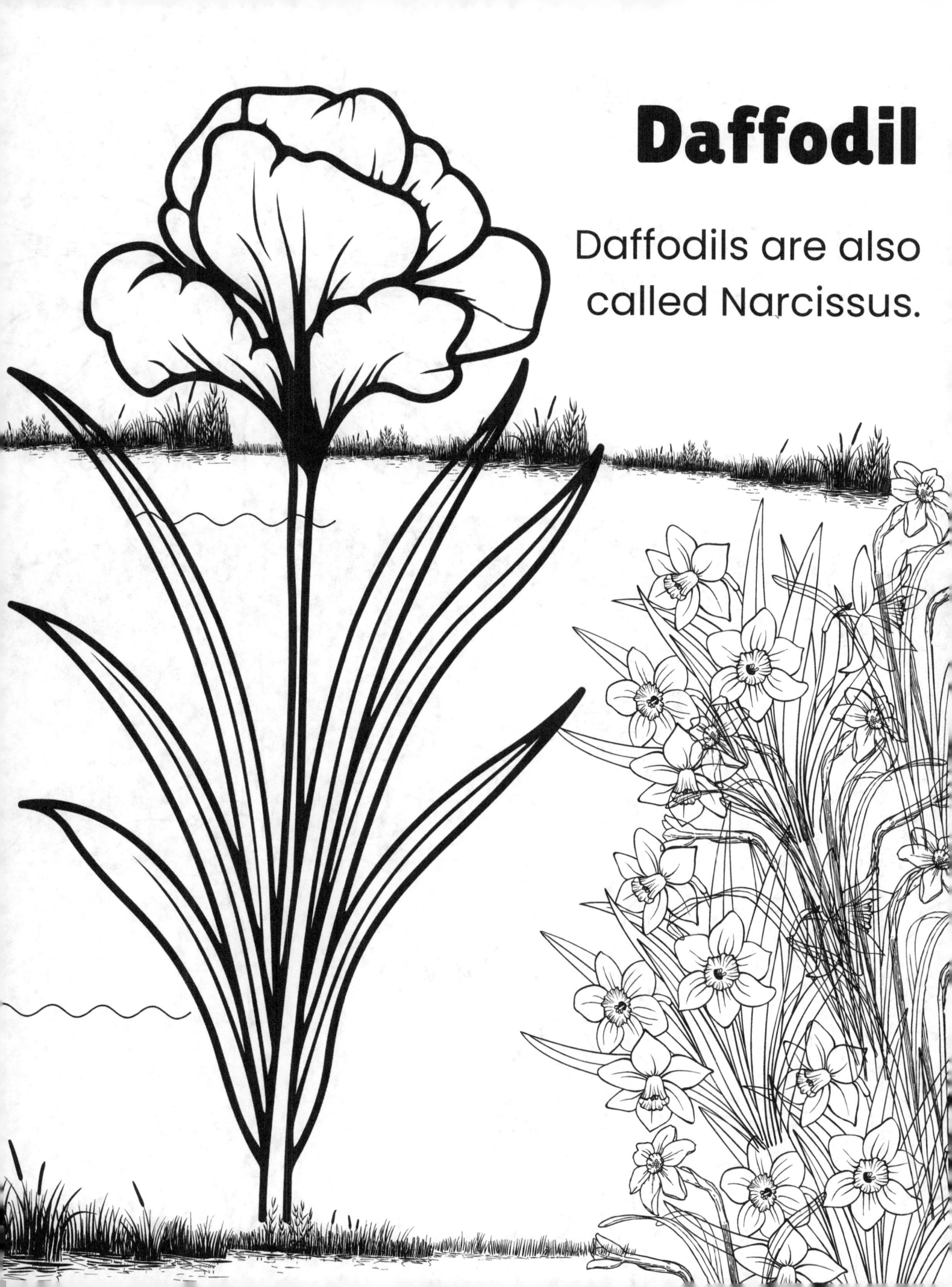

Sunflower

Sunflower seeds are
a delicious snack!

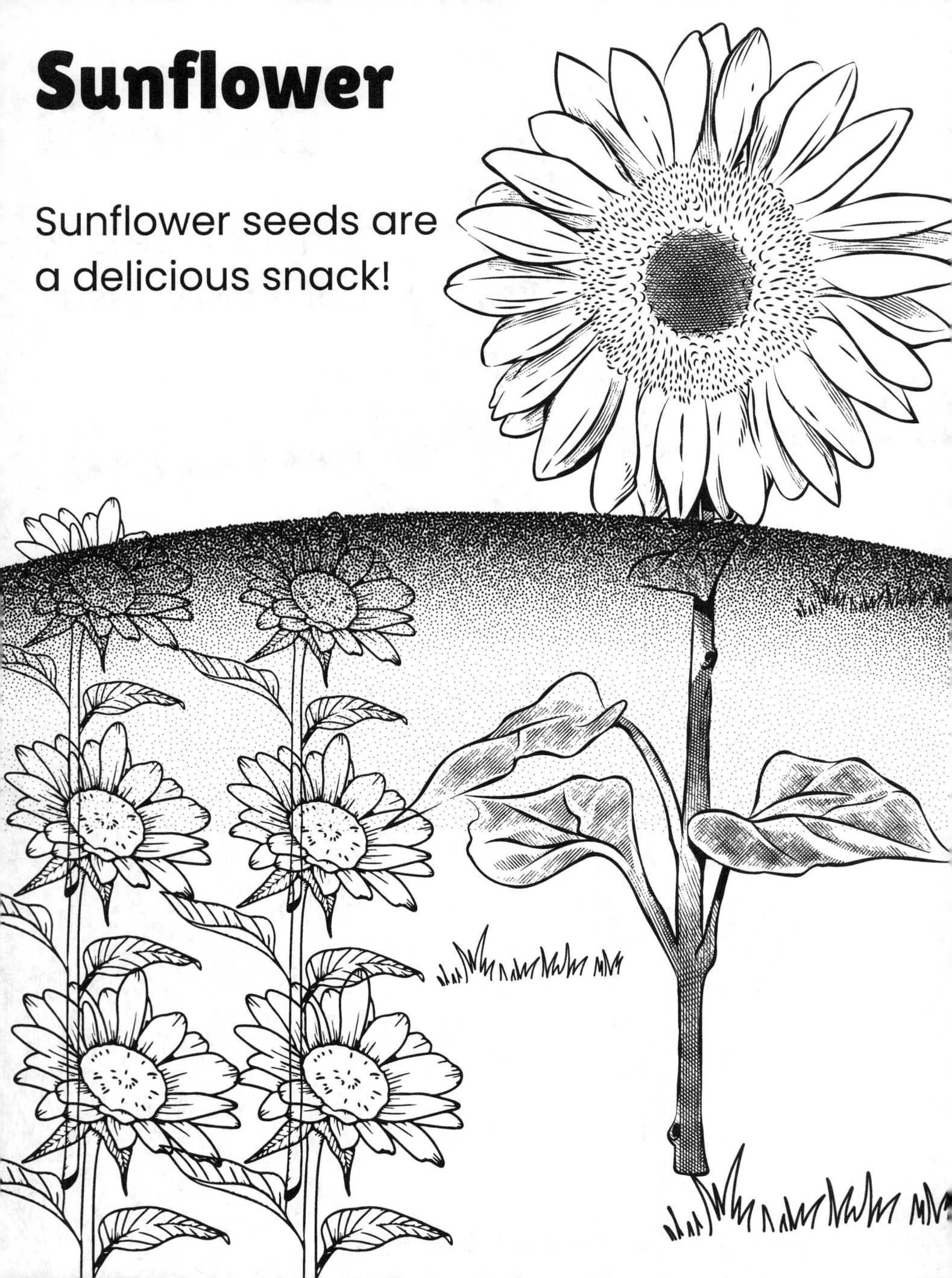

Tulip

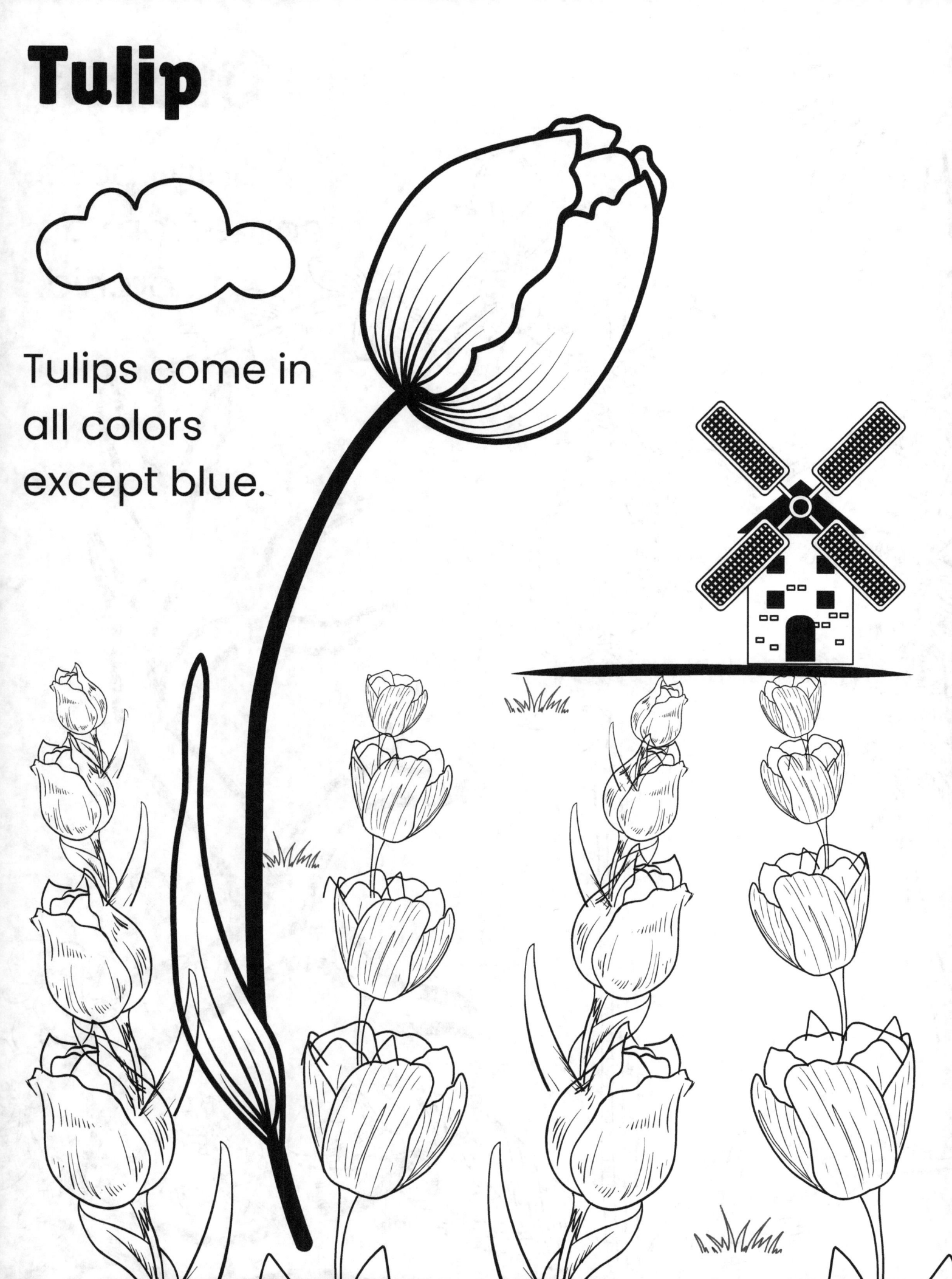

Tulips come in
all colors
except blue.

Orchid

Vanilla pods come from an orchid.

Daisy

Daisy flowers
and leaves
are edible.

Lilies are dangerous to cats.

Lily

Lavender

Not a flower but a plant, the lavender smell is used for rest and relaxing.

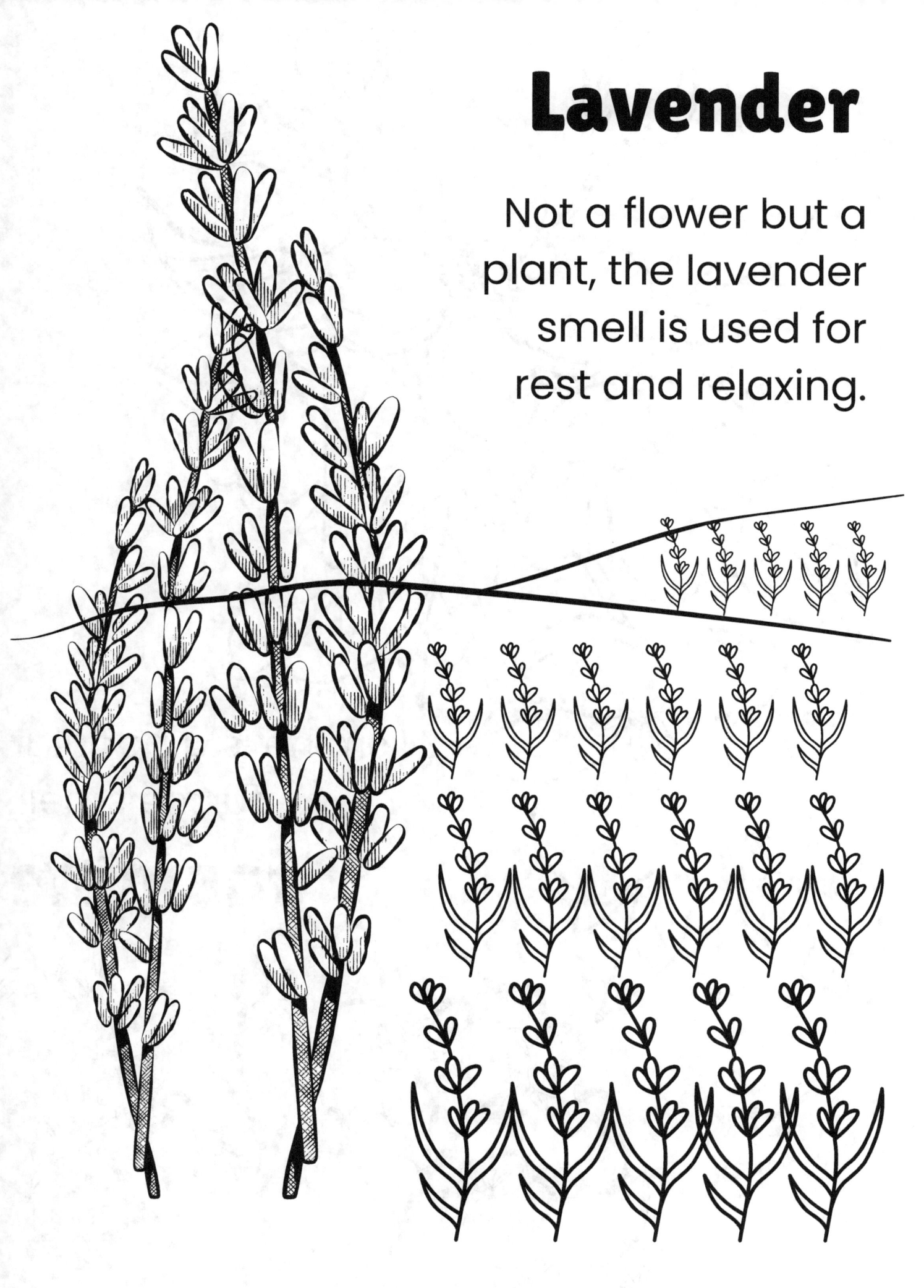

Jasmine is a popular perfurme smell.

Jasmine

Hibiscus

Hibiscus is the state flower of Hawaii.

Poppy

Poppies were used
in medicine back
in Ancient Egypt.

Iris

Iris means rainbow in Greek.

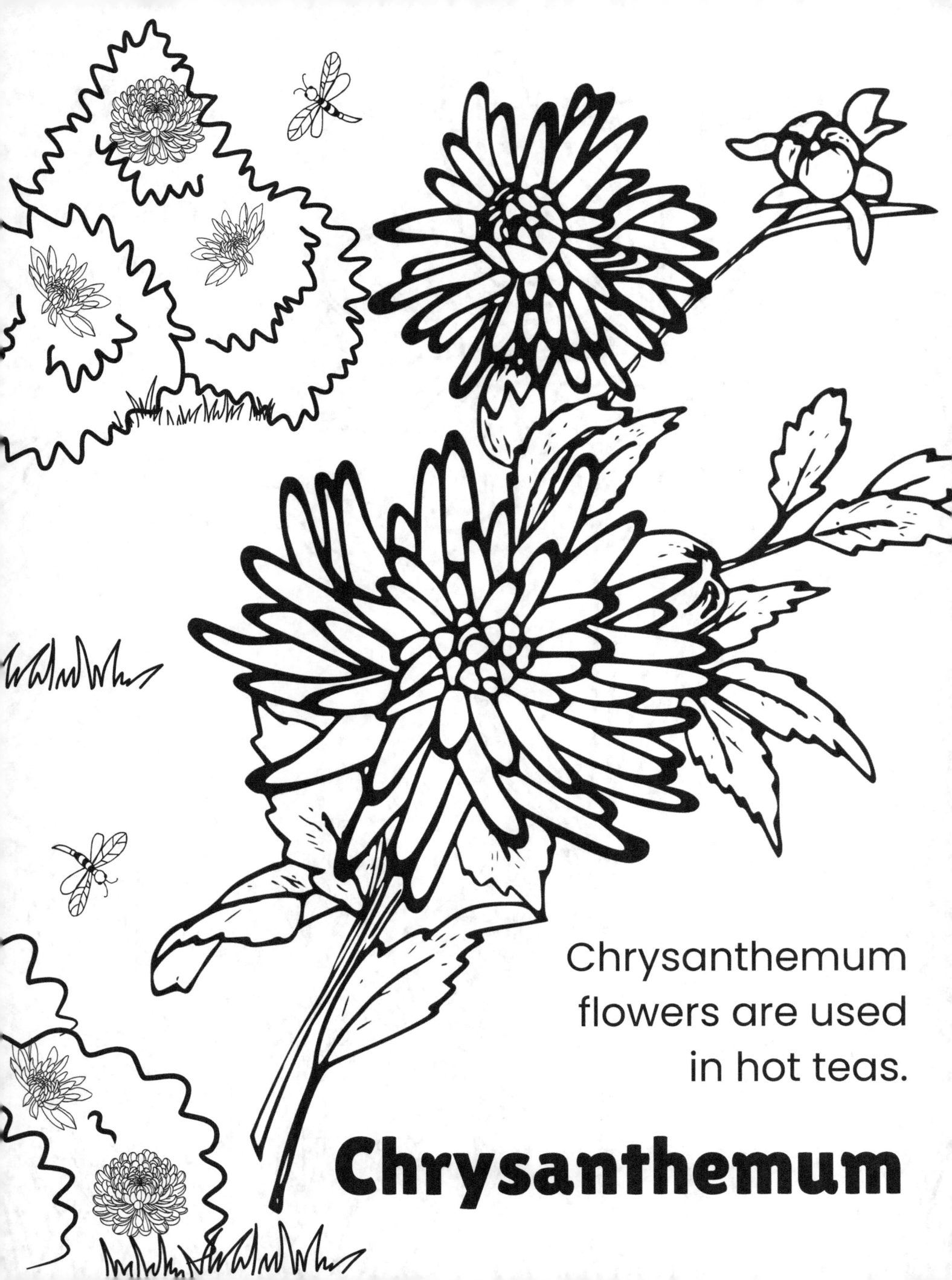

Chrysanthemum flowers are used in hot teas.

Chrysanthemum

Buttercup

Buttercup petals are shiny which help attract bees.

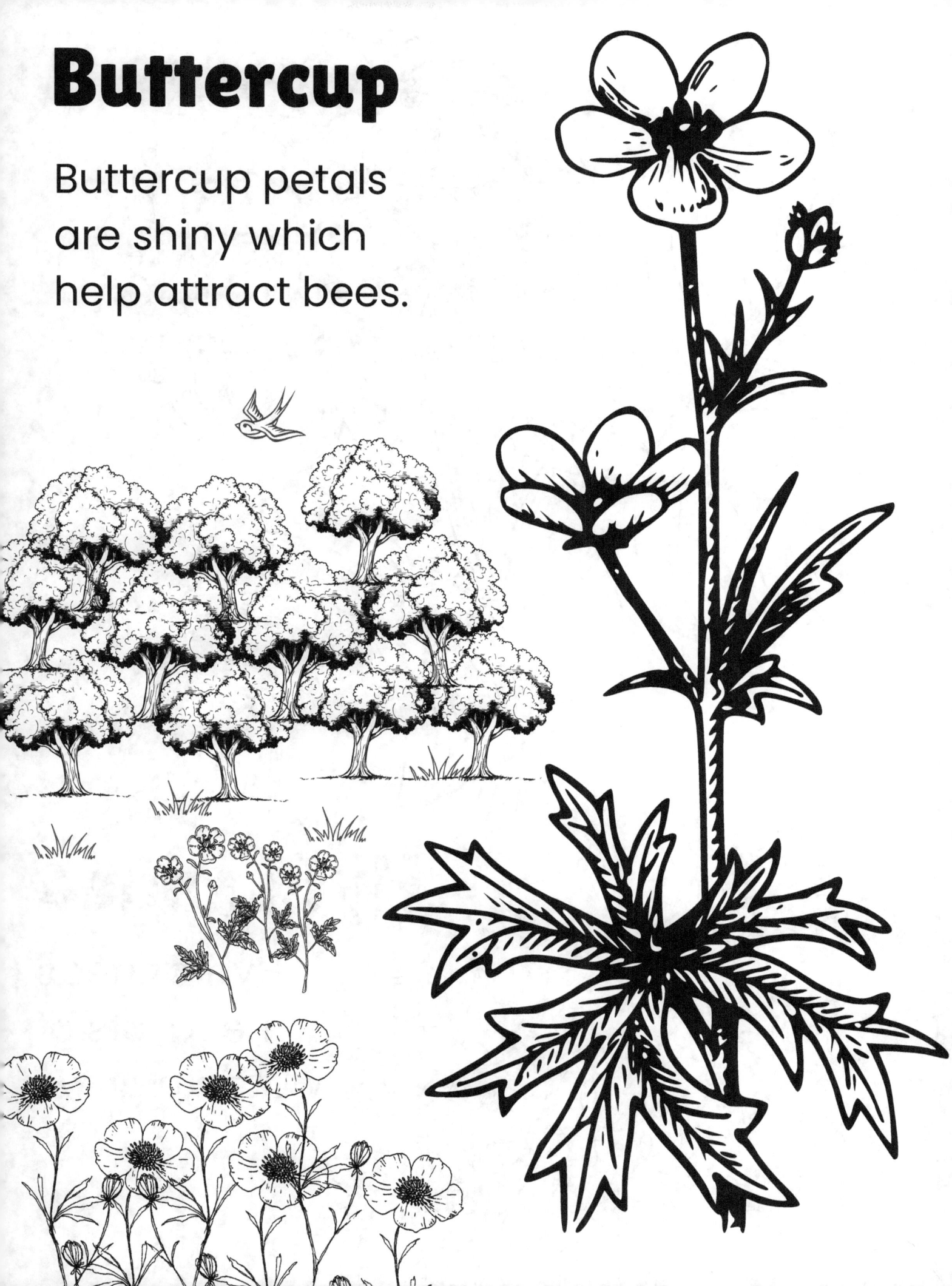

Hydrangea

Hydrangeas need lots of water to grow.

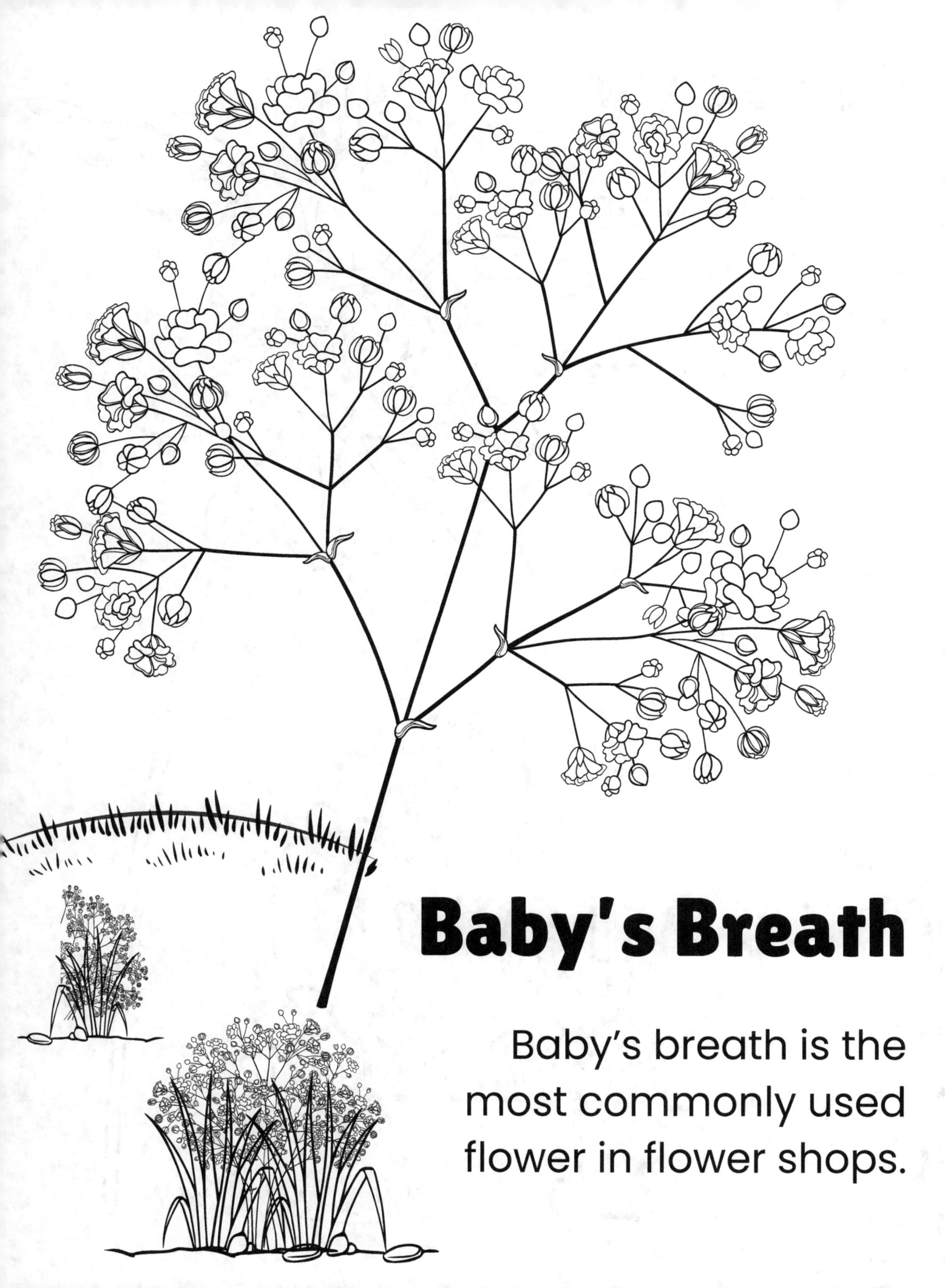

Baby's Breath

Baby's breath is the most commonly used flower in flower shops.

Gardenia

Gardenias have the strongest, sweetest smelling flowers.

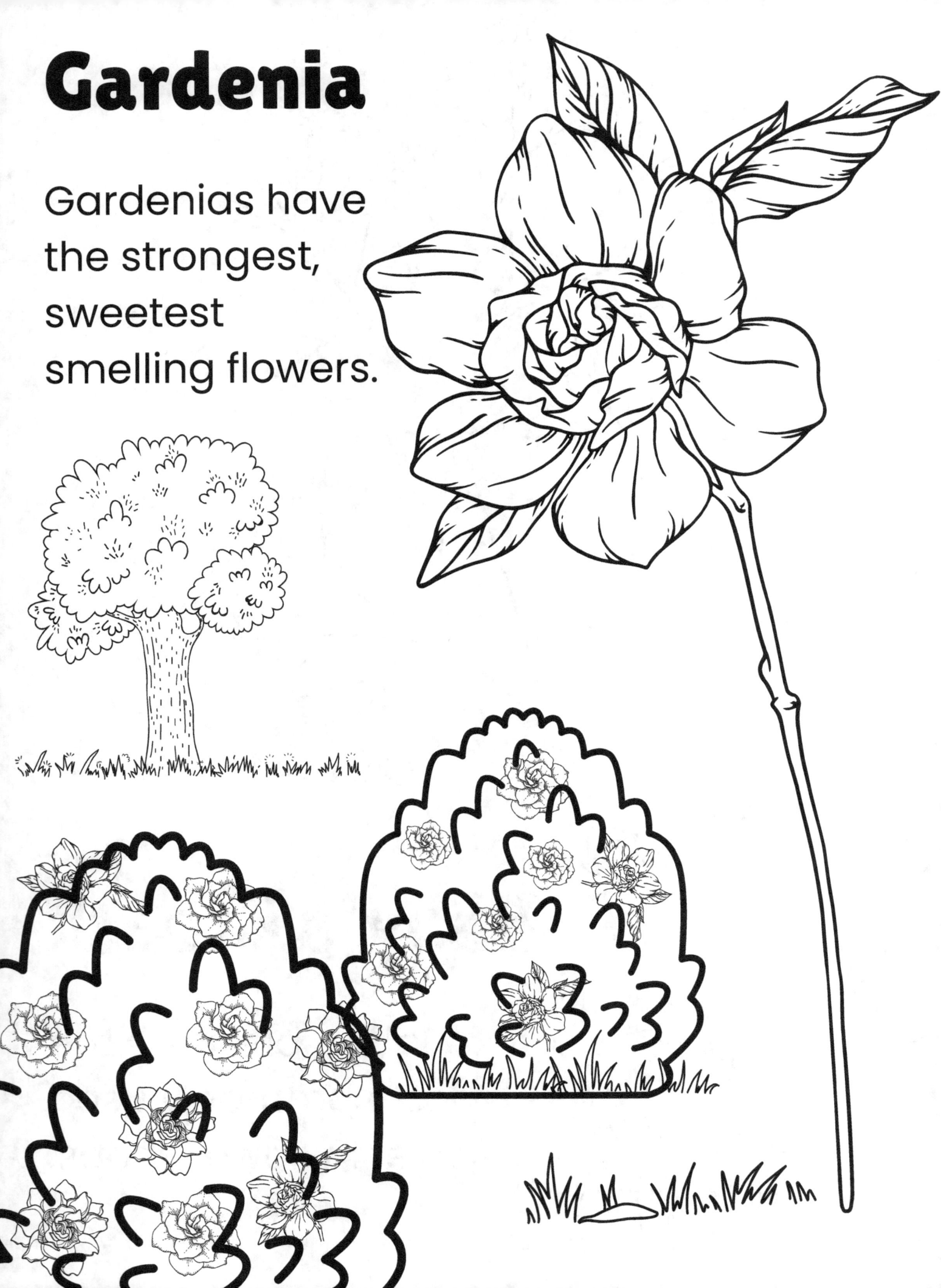

Lotus

A lotus is different
from a water lily.

The coolest thing I learned was

_____

_____

_____

_____

_____

What do you want to learn about next?

_____

_____

_____